# The Perfect Pet Owner

by Jen Malloy
illustrated by Cary Pillo

## SCHOLASTIC INC.

New York • Toronto • London • Auckland
Sydney • Mexico City • New Delhi • Hong Kong

ISBN 978-0-545-68606-8

Copyright © 2010 by Lefty's Editorial Services.

All rights reserved. Published by Scholastic Inc.

SCHOLASTIC, LET'S LEARN READERS™, and associated logos are trademarks and/or registered trademarks of Scholastic Inc.

12 11 10 9 8 7 6 5 4 3 2 1          14 15 16 17 18 19/0

Printed in China.

Meet Tina. Meet Tina's cat, Patches.
Meet Patches' new kittens!

**How many kittens did Patches have?**

The new kittens were all different. One kitten had lots of energy. It ran. It jumped. It chased its tail.

One kitten was very fancy. It had snow white fur and bright green eyes. It walked around like a proud princess.

 **How are the kittens on pages 4 and 5 different?**

One kitten was huge! It loved to eat and was nearly twice the size of the other kittens.

One kitten was teeny. It was sweet and shy. It liked to curl up on Tina's lap and purr.

**INFER**

**How does Tina feel about this kitten? How do you know?**

Tina's family could not take care of Patches plus all four kittens. Tina would have to find the kittens other homes. So she hung up a sign.

**INVESTIGATE**

**What does Tina's sign say?**

Tina hoped to find the perfect pet owner for each kitten. But she worried about the teeny one.

"Will someone want this itty-bitty kitten?" Tina asked.

"I'm sure you will find it a good home," said her mom.

Tina's sign worked! A boy named Jason stopped by. He was the tallest kid in Tina's class. Jason spent some time with the kittens.

"I'll take this one," he said, choosing the largest kitten.

**How are Jason and his kitten alike?**

Next, Tina's neighbor Sonia stopped by. She always wore pink and kept her hair neatly brushed. Sonia spent some time with the kittens.

"I'll take this one," she said, choosing the fancy kitten.

Two kids had stopped by. Two kittens were gone.

"No one has picked the teeny kitten," said Tina with concern.

"Don't worry," said her mom. "I'm sure you will find it a good home."

PREDICT

**Do you think the teeny kitten will find a good home?**

A while later, Tina's friend Matt showed up on his skateboard. He was always moving, moving, moving! Matt spent some time with the kittens.

"I'll take this one," he said, choosing the bouncy kitten.

Only the teeny kitten remained.

"I hope we can find the perfect pet owner for this one," said Tina.

"I know someone," said Tina's mom. "This person is caring, responsible, and kind."

"Who?" asked Tina.

"You!" said her mom with a smile.

Tina was so excited. She jumped up and down. She clapped her hands. Then Tina scooped up her new pet and gave it the perfect name: Teeny!

**TIE UP**

**Why is Teeny the perfect name for this kitten? What would you name it?**

# Story Prompts

Answer these questions after you have read the book.

**1** What is Tina like? Can you think of some great words to describe her?

**2** What adventures do Tina and Teeny have together? Turn on your imagination and tell a story about one.

**3** If you could get any pet in the world, what would you choose? Why?